NEW PLAYLIST

PITT POETRY SERIES

Terrance Hayes

Nancy Krygowski

Jeffrey McDaniel

Editors

NEW PLAYLIST

DAVID TRINIDAD

UNIVERSITY OF PITTSBURGH PRESS

Published by the University of Pittsburgh Press, Pittsburgh, Pa., 15260
Copyright © 2025, David Trinidad
All rights reserved
Manufactured in the United States of America
Printed on acid-free paper
10 9 8 7 6 5 4 3 2 1

ISBN 13: 978-0-8229-6740-8
ISBN 10: 0-8229-6740-5

Cover art: Jim Isermann, Untitled (1388), 1988. Enamel paint on panel and Orlon acrylic yarn, 96 × 96 × 2 inches. Collection of the Palm Springs Art Museum, purchased with funds provided by Herman & Faye Sarkowsky Charitable Foundation, Marilyn P. Loesberg, Donna J. MacMillian, Harold Matzner, Tom Minder, The Same & Diane Stewart Family Foundation, Helene V. Galen, Diane Rubin & Lenny Eber, and Roswitha Kima Smale, 2020.18a–b.

Cover design: Melissa Dias-Mandoly

As if the thing in doing were more dear
Than being done

—Paul Violi

CONTENTS

NEW PLAYLIST

Ode to Dusty Springfield

What makes
a voice
distinct?
What special
quality
makes it
indelible?
Yours is plaintive,
as any singer
of torch songs
must be,
yet endowed
with confidence,
and fully
in command.
Deep and
resonant,
a bit husky
if you like.
A voice that rises—
or skyrockets,
rather—from
a wellspring
of pure emotion.
Manically
infatuated
in "I Only
Want To Be
With You."
Desperate to
keep your
lover from
leaving in

"Stay Awhile."
Despondent
in "I Just
Don't Know
What To Do
With Myself"
and "You Don't
Have To Say
You Love Me."
All cried out
in "All Cried
Out." But then
amazingly
on the rebound
in "Brand New Me."

I hear your
voice, Dusty,
and I am
instantly
whisked
back in time,
not quite
a teenager
all over
again,
full of longing
and confusion,
listening
to your
latest hit
on my
red plastic

transistor
radio on
a mid-sixties
Los Angeles
suburban
summer
afternoon.

Twice in
my life, I
found myself
in the same
room as you.
Can one fathom
anything more
miraculous?
The first
time was
in 1983, late
November,
in the basement
of a church
in Los Feliz,
around the
corner from
where I lived.
Sober only
a few weeks,
I watched
you approach
the podium,
but didn't
realize who

you were
until you
identified
yourself as
"Dusty S."
For the next
twenty minutes,
you told us
the story
of your
drinking.
How early in
your career,
backstage
before a
performance,
one of the
Four Tops
handed you
your first
drink, vodka.
How smoothly
it went down
and loosened
you up,
lit you from
within,
gave you
enough
courage
to go out on
stage, into that
blinding spot,

and sing like
no one else.
The alcohol
eventually
stopped working—
it always does,
that brand
of magic
is transient—
and here you
were, two
decades
later, sober
and clean
and still singing,
so to speak,
before a live
audience.
In my youth,
your words
had come over
the radio
and stirred
feelings
of heartbreak
and infatuation.
Now they
inspired me
to keep
coming back.

The second
time, 1987,

four years
sober, at a more
upscale meeting
at Cedars-Sinai
in West Hollywood,
I sat directly
behind you.
It was hard
to breathe
being in such
close proximity.
I didn't hear
a word the
speaker said.
During his
drunkalog,
I slowly,
surreptitiously,
moved the
toe of my
white hightop
until it touched
the back of
your folding chair.
Then said a
little prayer.
I hoped
(should I be
embarrassed
admitting this?)
that some
of your
stardust

might travel
down the
metal leg
of your chair,
like a lightning
rod, and be
passed on
to me.

It's after
midnight
again, Dusty,
half a century
since, on
a suburban
lawn or alone
in my room,
I suffered
through hits
by Paul Revere
& the Raiders
and Herman's
Hermits,
just to
experience
two or
three minutes
of your
sultry voice.
I'm on
YouTube
again, watching
the black-and-white

video of you
singing "I
Only Want
To Be
With You."
Your 1964
appearance
on some teen
variety show.
I've viewed
it innumerable
times, but
it's always
exciting to see
you dance
out of the
darkness into
the round
spotlight,
exuberant
as the song's
intro, arms
outspread,
in chiffon
cocktail
dress and
high heels,
your platinum
hair, sprayed
perfectly
in place,
as bright
and shiny

as the moon.
Midway
through the
song—the
instrumental
bridge—you
turn and
sashay around
the edge of
the spotlight,
the ruffled
hem of your
chiffon dress
twisting with
your hips
and intricate
footwork.
Circle circling
circle: your
full backlit
hair orbiting
the pool of
white light
in the center
of the stage.
I watch this
again and again,
like Bashō's moon
walking around
the pond
all night long.

The Kiss

Proust

I never took my eyes off my mother.
I knew that when they were
at table I should not be permitted
to stay there for the whole
of dinner-time, and that Mamma,
for fear of annoying my father,
would not allow me to kiss her
several times in public, as I would
have done in my room. And so I
promised myself that in the dining-room,
as they began to eat and drink
and as I felt the hour approach,
I would put beforehand into this kiss,
which was bound to be so brief
and furtive, everything that
my own efforts could muster,
would carefully choose in advance
the exact spot on her cheek
where I would imprint it, and
would so prepare my thoughts
as to be able, thanks to these
preliminaries, to consecrate
the whole of the minute Mamma
would grant me to the sensation
of her cheek against my lips,
as a painter who can have his subject
for short sittings only, prepares
his palette, and from what he
remembers and from rough notes
does in advance everything which
he possibly can do in the sitter's
absence. But to-night, before the

dinner-bell had sounded, my
grandfather said with unconscious
cruelty: "The little man looks
tired; he'd better go up to bed.
Besides, we're dining late to-night."
And my father, who was less
scrupulous than my grandmother
or my mother in observing the letter
of a treaty, went on: "Yes; run along;
off to bed." I would have kissed
Mamma then and there, but at
that moment the dinner-bell rang.

All of the References to Beer in Bernadette Mayer's
The Desires of Mothers to Please Others in Letters

for Tony Trigilio

I'm drinking some awful cheap beer called Red White & Blue
made by Pabst

Demeter later invented beer.

Demeter's consequent invention of beer

Claire's picnic which was full of strangers and food, even
raspberries and chocolate cream pies and beer and ice cream

had a few beers

cans of beer

rolling rock!

I drink beer, sweet satchels of beer, some of it's bad beer

did I tell you how cheap cigarettes are in New Hampshire,
cigarettes and beer

I hid my beer, it was the Molson, the Octoberfest you gave me
hadn't been bad either

Bill C. is always saying, do you want another brewsky Bernie?

there are chemicals in the beer

beer

No Rheingold beer up here

To lose your job is to be free, only you can't get beer or beans

I feel guilty for drinking a few beers

you are forbidden from now on to drink any beer

It's colder outside than it is in the refrigerator so you can put the beer on the windowsill

We've had no real snow yet though we've stashed a supply of food, cigarettes and beer for being snowed in on this pretty echoing mountain.

the beers in gold cans

the beer capsizes on my cotton skirt

Molson Golden

The part of my house that keeps the beer coldest at this time of year is not the refrigerator

they write about cigarettes and beer and grass

if the beer freezes will the pipes

Golden England College mugs to drink beer from

I throw the beer bottle into the trash, it bangs against another one

WATER, BEER AND A DEER

I pride myself on drinking another beer at a time like this

Now Sophia's in a smaller box that says Michelob on it.

got the paper & some beer

TEN YEARS TILL THE NEXT BEER

taste of the metal beer

should I try a beer, will the beer lessen the chance for
contractions I aspire to tonight

Fourteen Moons

On the night of August 15, 1689, Bashō wrote fifteen poems about the moon. One of the haiku was subsequently lost, so now there are only fourteen. I've supplied the missing one.

Journey

Let's sleep all the way
to the palace
with the best view
of the full moon.

Crossing the Bridge at Asamutsu

From the bridge
mentioned by Sei Shōnagon
the moon drowns at dawn
in shallow water.

Forecast

If the sun is concealed
in the mountain's name,
tomorrow's moon
will be hidden by rain.

Complicated Pun

It is as difficult
to cover up the moon,
closer and brighter in autumn,
as a face scarred from smallpox.

Alive Again

This place has the same
name as another town
where a poet I admire
made the moon her own.

A Night at the Shrine

Eight times have I seen
through these pine trees
Kehi's famous moon.

Imperative

Don't thatch your roofs
with the reeds of Tamae
until you have taken in the moon.

According to Legend

A saint transplanted this sand
and on clear nights
you can pick up the moon
in your hands.

He Had a Tragic Life

When General Yoshinaka
woke from a bad dream
on this mountain
the moon made him sad.

What Do Innkeepers Know

The innkeeper predicted rain,
but that won't keep me
from pursuing
the harvest moon.

Where Is It?

That same innkeeper
told me a strange story
about a temple bell
being buried at the bottom of the sea.

Due to Rain

Not only did I miss
the moon, they've
now canceled the wrestling match
I really wanted to see.

Lost in Translation

The full moon makes me
long for the crescent moon
(which looks like a deer horn)
as well as the original name
of this old seaport.

After the Rain Has Cleared

I put on my robe
and go to the beach
and collect the many-colored shells
washed up by the moon.

The Lost Haiku

Snow-Viewing Party

Clouds part
and the lady arrives—
moonlight falling whitely
on her powdered brow.

The Pen

In all my years of collecting, there's only one thing I had as a child that I've not been able to find. A clear plastic sectional pen. Actually, it was more like a wand. About the length of a ruler. Each section was its own little pen—no longer than two inches— that could be pulled apart from the others. Lined up, they looked like miniature tubes of lipstick. Each filled with a different color ink: light blue, yellow, green, pink, purple, red. Because the plastic was transparent, you could see how much ink was left in each. Such anxiety when a particular color was about to run out! When you were done writing, you could stack all the sections together, back into a wand. It was the sort of thing you'd buy (with saved pennies) at a five-and-dime or drugstore. How I loved that pen. Fifth grade, the year I sat next to Terry Thrasher. At home at night, I imitated her girlish cursive—in light blue, in green, in red. Instead of dots, she drew circles over her i's. Her o's (at the end of words like "to" and "go") had an upward flourish, like an eyelash. Surely one pen, at the very least, still exists in the world. Perhaps in a box of old store stock, in a basement somewhere. Sitting there in the dark for half a century. Yet to be discovered and listed on eBay. And bought by me! The ink undoubtedly dried up—like in those dull Bic ballpoints I used in school. But still visible, some hopeful traces of purple, of yellow, of pink.

Clash Day

Junior High, 1966

It wasn't sanctioned by the school. Kids spread the word among themselves which day it would take place. Catch the principals and teachers off guard. The point was to wear clothes that intentionally clashed. Incompatible patterns (polka dots and paisley, plaids and stripes) and conflicting colors (purple and yellow, green and pink). Girls would braid *and* curl their hair. Boys would wear different colored socks. Some kids even showed up in mismatched shoes. A relief not to care, for a day, how you looked. To let go of the pressure to be perfect, or at least not be singled out as flawed—too pimply, too effeminate, too overweight. Another secret whispered by students: If you wore red and black on Friday, it meant you were a "whore." Those were the days when teachers and administrators could lay hands on you. I once offended a substitute teacher during a dictionary exercise, by blurting out a certain three-letter word. "Tit." Which elicited laughs from the class. She sent me to the vice principal's office for punishment. He had me bend over a desk and then swatted me with a wooden paddle. Once. Twice. Three times. The word was in the dictionary, was all I could say in my own defense. I'm sure I glared at that substitute with pure hatred when I returned to class. Which was held, I distinctly remember, in one of the bungalows next to the P.E. field.

All Things Must Pass

Amy texts to tell me the Cinerama Dome in Hollywood is about to close. Pang of regret. Gone forever, the only concrete geodesic dome in the world. The last time I was there was in the late nineties, with Dennis. We saw *The Fifth Element*. I had an early flight the next morning and was worried about not getting enough sleep. I saw *2010: The Year We Make Contact* there in the mid-eighties, with my A.A. friend Mark. At the climax, when Jupiter contracts and explodes, I had an anxiety attack, had to step out into the lobby. Newly sober, I was always on edge. In the mid-seventies I saw *Barry Lyndon* there, and was bored. Decades later I saw it again, on VHS, and realized what a great movie it is. I wish I'd appreciated it on the big screen.

some chance / of being hallowed

Underlined in my copy of Randall Mann's A Better Life

The long slide,
a B-side
play-
list

of degradation

*

Get off
my
intellectual
property.

*

Living
Dead
giving
head.

*

Local fame.

*

psalms on men's washroom stalls

*

Time to borrow
a Marlboro

*

Sequins
on a gown.

*

and who
doesn't
catwalk
a conference
room?

*

Poster-boys of childhood gone.

*

The phones of the dead chirp.

Sylvia Plath's Recipe Cards

for Amy Gerstler, on her birthday

Shirley Norton's Potato Refrigerator Rolls
Easy-Mix French Dressing
Fruit Drink
Oatmeal Cookies
Sour Milk Gingerbread
Toll House Cookies
Mayonnaise
Scottish Fancies
Cherry & Cottage Cheese Cobbler
Ted's Mother's Scots Porridge Oats Biscuits[1]
3 Loaves Dot's Carrot Cake
Apfelkuchen[2]
Dido's Roast Chicken[3]
Beef Stew
Broiled Cape Scallops
Vanilla Nut Cookies
Dream Bars (Aunt Elizabeth's)
Aurelia's Apple Crisp
Chocolate Brownies
Frosted Cookies
Grammy's "Drop Molasses Cookies"[4]
Date-Nut Bars
Dot's Meat Loaf
Scotch Macaroons
Sponge Cake
Dot's Orange Cookies
Tomato-Soup Spice Cake[5]
Easy-Mix Pie Crust
Apple Filling
Clara's Basic Yeast Dough
Streusel Cake
Cinnamon Rolls

Grammy's Fish Chowder
Chicken Fricassee[6]

1. "These are the most delicious cakes I know about. (Ted's own words written from London.)"
2. Apple Cake
3. "Serve with unripe bananas fried in butter (& saffron rice if you want to be flossie)."
4. Aurelia: "(I doubt that I ever made these cookies for you and Warren. Grammy made them for her children and we liked them very much.)"
5. Aurelia: "You used to like an orange icing on this—about 2 tablespoons of butter creamed, icing sugar and orange juice. To make it special, I used to place walnut halves or quarters on the icing so that, when cut in squares, each square would have a piece of nut in the center."
6. Aurelia: "Dump flour and stock simultaneously into melted margarine and stir rapidly with that wiry spoon-thing Mrs. Cantor gave you."

Hidden Picture

Try to find
Sharon Tate in
the party scene
in *Rosemary's Baby.*

Queen of the Lot

When was the last time I watched *The Letter*—early '40s film noir melodrama starring Miss Bette Davis? She shoots her lover, is acquitted, then gets stabbed to death at the end by her dead lover's wife—played by the great Gale Sondergaard, who, as I recall, doesn't say a word. A seething silent performance. Clouds moving across the full moon, moonlight filtering through slatted blinds—indelible black-and-white images, old Hollywood magic. When was the last time I read poems by John Wieners, who so often evokes the movie queens of yesteryear? Why, just this morning!

Claim to Fame

He was a professional figure skater.
He was a broom in "Fantasia on Ice."

Gowns by Adrian

for Robyn Schiff

He designed the costumes for most of the movies she made at
MGM. Miles of beribboned white ruffles. Hooded, fur-trimmed
capes and tasseled velveteen trains. Billowing clouds of sequin-
studded tulle. Extravagance was his style, but no amount of
fabric (or feathers or flowers or jewels) could upstage Garbo's
ethereal presence, or that face. Rather, his creations gave her
the emotional key to her characters: women overcome with
passion, temptresses, doomed adulteresses, Nordic queens. Theirs
was a perfect collaboration. They once spent hours together,
working out a "taffeta problem." A thin layer of silk lining,
they discovered, would prevent the microphone from picking
up the swish. Who else shared this kind of intimacy with the
reclusive star (labeled "the Swedish Sphinx" by the press). Only
the camera (for close-ups). And mustachioed John Gilbert (her
lover offscreen and on). In 1941, Adrian prepared sketches for
Two-Faced Woman (no one knew it would be Garbo's final film).
He later described one of the concoctions: "suntan soufflé over
the same shade of lining, gathered skirt, gold-lace belt with lace
coming up the front." Louis B. Mayer nixed the designs. He
insisted on something more austere. The world was at war, after
all: Not a time for extravagance. As a result, Adrian tendered
his resignation. The mogul was taken aback. He couldn't believe
anyone would leave Metro of their own accord. On his last day
at the studio, Adrian went to Garbo's dressing room to bid her
farewell. "What shall I give you to remember me by?" she asks as
Marguerite Gautier in *Camille*. "You can't give me the only thing
I'd like," replies her ardent suitor. "What?" "A tear." "I'm very
sorry that you're leaving," Garbo told Adrian, "but, you know, I
never really liked most of the clothes you made me wear." Was
she sincere, or merely deflecting her hurt? Adrian confided his
to Irene Selznick. He'd never know (he died of a heart attack in
1959, at age fifty-six) that Garbo kept, for the rest of her life, his

parting gift: a pair of mauve kid gloves she had worn in *Camille*. The gloves were embroidered with vines of seed pearls and tiny steel beads, that secretly intertwined into the actress' initials. "I'm not always sincere," she says in that very film. "One can't be in this world, you know."

Periwinkle Blue

A Crayola crayon. And the color Mrs. Bates was buried in.
"I helped Norman pick out the dress." Once, after a poetry
reading, a friend (who was grieving the loss of his partner) told
me he saw, when I was standing at the podium, my aura. It was
periwinkle blue.

Kay Francis

The diary of a movie star. What could be more glamorous. But not for the reasons you'd suppose. It was among the papers she donated to the Museum of the City of New York in 1968 (the year of her death). Much of the diary is in shorthand, and had to be decoded. She chronicles her love affairs, yes. And her friendships with gay men (her studio reportedly paid one of them to keep her out of mischief). But it turns out she was underwhelmed by stardom. Which makes her a heroine in my book. "To earn it by disdaining it," says Emily Dickinson, "Is Fame's consummate Fee." Not that Francis was ungrateful (she was one of the highest-paid actresses in the first half of the 1930s, the worst years of the Depression), she just didn't like getting up at 5:45 a.m. to be fitted for evening gowns. "I can't wait to be forgotten," she wrote in her diary. With perfect, as Marianne Moore would say, contempt. What could be more glamorous than that.

Garden

March 20, 2022 First day of spring. From downstairs window, after opening blinds: squirrel perched atop fence, red-breasted robin pecking at wet stone-tiles.

Gone already: the clump of little purple flowers that Michael Robins commented on when he visited last week. I told him: "Whenever I see the first flowers, I think, 'Persephone's back.'"

March 21 Warm today—high of 68. Warm enough to wear shorts.

More dead leaves than green. Still recovering from what I would call an intense Chicago winter. White was all the rage.

When sunlight hits the garden, I am aware of green sprouts. And a few small purple flowers, like the previous clump—purple with yellow stamens. And in the distance: sirens.

Later: A cardinal alit in bare branches. So vivid. It let me admire it for the longest time.

March 22 It's not my garden, by the way, but my landlord's. A communal space between a three-flat and a coach house, where I live. Two brown plastic Adirondack chairs. Small round weather-beaten wooden end table. Several large planters in the shape of Grecian urns. The space mostly unused (so it usually feels like mine), though sometimes, in summer, neighbors will sit in the brown chairs. Michael sat in one last Thursday, while he waited for me to pee and turn on my alarm system. Then we walked through Andersonville. Stopped at Rattleback Records, where I bought Joni Mitchell's *Hejira* and Patti Smith's *Wave*. Then Women & Children First, where Michael bought (with a gift certificate from Abigail Zimmer) Diane Seuss' *frank: sonnets*. He said it had just won the NBCC award.

On the street we ran into Daniel Borzutsky and Rachel Galvin. In a carriage: their four-month-old baby, Felix. On a leash: a big happy white dog named Gizmo. Daniel was wearing sunglasses and a powder blue T-shirt. He said he was at the Zoom reading I did for

UIC last October. Then Michael and I walked through St. Boniface Cemetery. One lap around the outer edge, which equals one mile.

March 23 After two days of rain, there should soon be some action in the garden.

Birds (rather than people) are tweeting.

Among the wet leaves: a sad-looking stone angel. It used to sit in the crotch of the tree with three trunks, but fell out at some point. So I guess it's a fallen angel.

March 24 Overcast—more rain expected.

Squirrel—flouncing around.

I googled the little purple flowers with the yellow stamens (all gone now), and discovered their name: *Crocus tommasinianus*. A native to the hillsides and woodland areas of southern Hungary into the northern Balkans (don't you love the sound of Wiki-ese), it is commonly called snow crocus because it is one of the earliest of the crocuses to bloom. These pale lavender, goblet-shaped flowers appear in late winter to early spring (March in St. Louis). And in Chicago! Its genus name, *krokos*, comes from the ancient Greek. It is one of the most ancient plant names. Why do I find that comforting? Something in "my" garden reaches all the way back to antiquity.

March 25 Woken at 6:00 a.m. (two hours before my alarm) by sounds of birds. One rat-a-tat-tatting like a machine gun. Another producing a series of trills and whistles. Then came the rumble of a dump truck, in the alley behind my coach house.

March 26 Frost on the rooftop this morning, and now snow flurries. The brown Adirondack chairs are beginning to turn white. And I thought winter was over! When it comes to nature, I've always been naïve. (A nice way of saying "ignorant.")

March 27   Bird call: two whistles, followed by six clucks. This morning I let that be my snooze alarm.

At 9:11: a siren.

Chill breeze, but sunny. Maybe now we'll start to see some flowers.

March 28   More sun. Just keep that light on.

March 29   I wish I knew the name of every tree, flower, and plant in the garden. As Elizabeth Bishop put it in her last notebook: "I want now — now that it's too late — to learn the name of *everything*."

I know the name of every girl group from the 1960s. The name of every Barbie outfit (and the accessories they came with). The movies of certain actresses. The poems of certain poets. Every film noir. In high school I memorized all the Oscar winners and nominees, from almost every category (up until 1970). Most of that knowledge is gone (like my high school French). Can the mind only hold so much at one time? D.A. Powell possesses an encyclopedic knowledge of Oscar trivia. We often, in our late-night phone conversations, play Oscar guessing games.

You can know everything about anything if you have the time, the inclination, the focus. If it's an obsession. But how long will you hold onto it? Sooner or later it begins to fade. Especially if replaced by new obsessions.

Obsession du jour: pre-Code Hollywood movies.

March 30   Yesterday, around the block on Hollywood Avenue, in someone's flower bed, I saw the first daffodil. No such forerunners in the garden I open my blinds to each morning.

It's expected to rain all day today.

Last year Michael told me (we were walking in St. Boniface Cemetery) about an app that will identify trees. You just hold your phone up to the tree and it tells you what it is. Like a song on Shazam. There are other apps for identifying flowers and birds and whatnot. Last week I texted Michael about this. His reply: "The app is called PictureThis. Use the free version and, while using the app, look for the tiny x in the corner to close the pop-ups that want you to buy a paid version."

I've yet to download it. Can't really see myself walking around the garden holding my phone up to every tree, every plant. It would feel like cheating somehow.

March 31 There used to be a forsythia in a corner by the front gate. A few years ago Roland, my landlord, took it out. I miss that splash of bright yellow. I knew it was a forsythia because of Tim Dlugos' poem "Pretty Convincing." I once did a close reading of it with my graduate students. We looked up every word and reference we didn't understand. In that class we also did a close reading of a poem by James Schuyler. During which one of the students moaned, "No more flowers!"

April 1 From an old journal: "Increasingly, I long to know the names of flowers, plants, trees—so I can identify and describe them. Perhaps I can get a few books, or study them online." Wrote this on May 10, 2009. Clearly my desire to know nature has taken a back seat to more pressing obsessions. Guess I'd rather watch movies than trees.

And yet this, also from an old journal: May 1, 2011: "Color in the garden: 1 red tulip, 2 orange tulips, pink something, white something (small tree with thin floppy blossoms), 2 daffodils, 2 full purple plants (rhododendrons?), pink bleeding hearts,* 4 yellow tulips, yellow bush in bloom in corner near gate.** More to come: clusters of green bulb leaves shooting up."

*I was later told by a friend that these are not bleeding hearts (*Lamprocapnos spectabilis*) but lady's slippers (*Cypripedium reginae*). After a little googling, I realize he was wrong. They are indeed bleeding hearts. (Said friend was a bit of a know-it-all.) The bleeding heart is also known as lyre flower, heart flower, and lady-in-a-bath.
** forsythia

April 2   This sense of expectancy, on the verge of something about to happen, of more to come . . .
Jane Kenyon: "More flowers, more art."

Connect the Dots

Peg Entwistle was the young woman who, in 1932, at the age of twenty-four, threw herself off of the Hollywood Sign. Her suicide inspired the Dory Previn song "Mary C. Brown and the Hollywood Sign," which I listened to a lot in the early 1970s, when I was around the age Peg Entwistle was when she jumped to her death. She'd climbed a workman's ladder to the top of the "H," a height of forty-five feet. The fictional movie in the Netflix miniseries *Hollywood* (first *Peg*, then retitled *Meg*) is based on Peg Entwistle's life and death. I gave up on *Hollywood* after the fourth episode because I couldn't stand all the historical inaccuracies. It was like watching a parallel politically correct universe. Which could have been fun if it weren't so disrespectful to Rock Hudson (portrayed as dumber than a doornail) and Peg Entwistle (who was a real person who suffered real pain). In her song, Dory Previn changes Peg's name, and speculates she jumped because "she did not become a star." And vents her own disillusionment with Tinseltown. As a lyricist, she'd written songs for movies. One of them, *Inside Daisy Clover*, which I watched on the late show as a teenager, was about a movie star's disillusionment with Hollywood. Daisy is played by Natalie Wood. She attempts suicide, then ends up blowing up her beach house instead. I share Natalie Wood's birthday: July 20. In the late 1920s, Peg Entwistle was briefly married to actor Robert Keith. Keith failed to tell her he had a son by a previous marriage. Entwistle cited this deceit, along with charges of cruelty, when she filed for divorce. The son, Brian Keith, grew up to be a successful actor. I watched him, when I was a child, in *The Parent Trap*, a Disney film in which Hayley Mills plays identical twins who trade places in order to bring their divorced parents back together. I loved the idea of being able to switch identities, of pretending to be someone else. In the seventies, two different men at two different gay bars told me that I reminded them of Natalie Wood. This solidified my astrological "twinship" with the glamorous star.

After appearing in several Broadway productions, Peg Entwistle made her way to Hollywood in 1932. She was cast in her one and only film, *Thirteen Women*, a thriller produced by David O. Selznick and starring Myrna Loy and Irene Dunne. After the movie performed poorly for test audiences, Entwistle's screen time was cut from sixteen to four minutes. According to urban myth, this disappointment is what led her to suicide. *Thirteen Women* opened one month after Entwistle's death. Recently, when I watched the DVD, I wished it were possible to see those twelve missing minutes. My friend Doug and I are watching and discussing, as a lark, the first six Johnny Weissmuller Tarzan movies. (I can think of worse ways of spending one's Saturday nights.) The British actor John Buckler appears in the third (*Tarzan Escapes*) as Captain Fry, the attractive but ultimately treacherous leader of an expedition to Tarzan's jungle home. At the end of the movie (spoiler alert), Fry falls into a quicksand bog and is swallowed up. I thought Buckler handsome enough to google, and learned (shockingly) that he died at the age of thirty. On October 30, 1936, Buckler and his actor father Hugh were drowned in Malibu Lake when their automobile skidded off the road during a rainstorm and overturned in the water. *Tarzan Escapes* was his sixth and final film; he died one week before its release. Natalie Wood drowned, in a terrible accident, in November 1981, in the dark water off Catalina Island. I had a panic attack when I saw the news on TV. On the Wikipedia page for Hugh Buckler, there is a picture of the cast of the 1931 Broadway production of George Bernard Shaw's *Getting Married*. Among the ten actors are Buckler and (surprise) Peg Entwistle. A pretty blonde ingenue in a stylish white wedding dress. In 1932, the Hollywood Sign was the Hollywoodland Sign. Advertising left over from a housing development in the Hollywood Hills. A woman hiking near the sign found one of Entwistle's shoes, and her purse, and her jacket. In the purse was a suicide note, and in the ravine below, Entwistle's body. The coroner reported the cause of death as multiple fractures of the pelvis. "I am sorry for everything," Peg wrote in her note, "If I had done this a long time ago, it would have saved a lot of pain." On the Wikipedia page for *Tarzan Escapes*, it says that a scene which took a week to shoot, featuring Tarzan fighting vampire bats, was cut from the final film after test audiences found it too intense. I would have liked to have seen that scene.

For Sylvia

On the sidewalk: a red button.

From the train: a graveyard covered in snow.

30 I Remembers

for James Cushing

I remember the earthquake preparedness kit I kept in the trunk
of my car when I lived in Los Angeles. I'd attended a (mandatory)
lecture at my (city) job about how bad it was going to be when the
big one hit. It scared me enough that I went out and bought a gallon
bottle of drinking water, a flashlight and batteries, first aid kit, etc.

I remember stubbing my toe on the driveway of my childhood home.

I remember submitting poems to *Poetry* magazine in the nineties,
and the editor at the time (Joseph Parisi) writing back, "I just can't
bring myself to publish you."

I remember the plastic decorations on birthday cakes, that you could
keep afterwards as toys: baseball players and golfers, pirate ships
and treasure chests, Cinderella's gilt carriage, telephone teens, hula
dancers and palm trees, ballerinas in arabesque.

I remember before seatbelts. And my mother (at the wheel)
extending her right arm to protect me (in the passenger seat) when
we came to an abrupt stop.

I remember the lemon meringue pies my mother used to make—
from scratch. The vibrant yellow filling. The glazed, cloud-like white
peaks (delicately browned in places). The slightly crumbly homemade
crust. A slice looked perfect, like a painting by Wayne Thiebaud, like
pop art.

I remember Janet Gray's book *A Hundred Flowers*. Each poem
inspired by a different flower painting in a Georgia O'Keeffe
coffee-table book. My favorite was the one that likened the folds of
O'Keeffe's white petals to Marilyn Monroe's creased bedsheets.

I remember how scary *Jaws* was the first time I saw it in the mid-seventies. Swimming in the ocean would never again be as fun.

I remember roasting marshmallows in the fireplace at John and Eula's house. With several rambunctious children. And Suzanne saying to them, "Fire is not a toy."

I remember the eerie glamour of a suburban midnight. And the wind blowing through trees in the dark. And that sense of solitude while the rest of the world slept.

I remember ghosts coming out of portraits in the Haunted Mansion at Disneyland. And ghost couples waltzing in the ballroom. And ghosts flying out of gravestones. And the three ghosts trying to thumb a ride at the end.

I remember wistfully listening to my single of "Moon River" (the theme song from *Breakfast at Tiffany's*) and wishing I could be as free a spirit as Holly Golightly.

I remember not being able to look at the newspaper until my father was finished with it. And asking him repeatedly, "Are you done with the movie section?"

I remember when I first moved from New York to Chicago, sitting with Joris on the grass at the lakefront, looking up at a pure blue September sky. And at the Emerald City-esque cluster of buildings downtown. And thinking: "Chicago is great for me, for now. But it's not forever."

I remember sparklers and firecrackers and Roman candles and whistlers and black snakes and cherry bombs and the little log cabin with smoke pouring out of it.

I remember how much I loved Greek myths. Sisyphus perpetually pushing the stone up a mountain in Hades. Daphne turning into a tree. Atlas holding the universe on his shoulders. Pandora opening the box and unleashing all the ills on the world.

I remember the poets who taught at Cal State Northridge when I was a student there in the seventies: Robert Deutsch, Arthur Lane, Benjamin Saltman, Ann Stanford.

I remember what Carol Muske-Dukes said about Ann Stanford's poems, that they were written to last, and thinking what a high compliment that was.

I remember the strange texture (rough) of old-fashioned ceramic dolls.

I remember the metal breadbox on our pink kitchen counter. And the coffee cups (half a dozen or so) hooked by their handles on a little "tree."

I remember the names of Crayola crayons: Goldenrod, Midnight Blue, Periwinkle, Carnation Pink, Burnt Sienna, Raw Umber. And the "metallic" shades—Gold, Silver, Copper—that had a sparkle to them. And the built-in sharpener on the back of the box. And peeling away the label as each crayon got shorter.

I remember wishing in earnest as I tossed the coin into the well.

I remember my first part-time job, at McDonald's. I was still in high school. With a child-sized broom, I had to sweep the trash in the parking lot into a long-handled dustpan. Which I found humiliating. Especially when kids from my school would drive through and order food. I lasted two weeks.

I remember my great-aunt Louise, who loved murder mysteries, and who once she learned I aspired to write, would ever after ask, "When are you going to write me a mystery?"

I remember the little wooden spoons that came with ice cream cups (vanilla with chocolate or strawberry swirls).

I remember, in old movies, the days flying off of a calendar, to indicate the passage of time.

I remember the talking flowers in Disney's *Alice in Wonderland*. The roses and pansies and tiger lilies that were really tigers. The iris that was a snobbish, big-bosomed dowager with pince-nez. And how they turned on Alice when they thought she was a weed.

I remember that the song "Eye in the Sky" was playing on the radio in the taxi when I first saw the skyline of New York City.

I remember looking into dioramas. And toy theaters. And dollhouses. With utter wonder.

I remember when I thought thirty was old.

Never Argue with the Movies

1

In *To the Last Man*, a 1933 Western
about feuding families, Randolph Scott
is trying to get on with Esther Ralston
(unschooled and pretty wild). She
"ain't used to being polite at." He notices
that she's not wearing shoes. "It must
be sort of hard going barefoot through
these mountains." She takes offense:
"It's none of your business that I ain't
got shoes and stockin's." "I didn't mean
anything that way. They write poems
about barefoot girls like you." "What's
a poem?" she asks belligerently. "Oh,
a lot of words put together. They don't
mean anything, but they sound pretty good."

2

In *The Lives of a Bengal Lancer*, a 1935
adventure film, Gary Cooper and Franchot
Tone have both been tortured (bamboo
shoots under fingernails) and imprisoned
in a cell. Neither of them cracked under
pressure; they're true heroes. Shortly before
the explosive finale, Tone quotes Lewis Carroll:
"'The time has come,' the Walrus said, /
'To talk of many things: / Of shoes—and ships—
and sealing-wax— / Of cabbages—and kings—'"
"Oh, shut up!" barks Coop. "You don't like
poetry?" "How should I know, I never read any."

3

In *Evelyn Prentice*, a 1934 crime drama,
Myrna Loy receives a book in the mail
from a supposed admirer (actually a gigolo)
she met at a nightclub. *"Bonjour,"* says
her friend Una Merkel when she joins her
for breakfast. (Her French is a charming
affectation.) "Don't tell me you go in for
early morning reading. What's the book?"
"It's called *Sonnets to the Sun,*" replies Loy.
"What to the which?" *"Sonnets to the Sun.*
Pretty, isn't it? It's a book of poems." "Poems?
In the morning? Darling, it's your liver."
Loy reads her the letter that came with it.
"Oh, the good-looking thrill with broad
shoulders," coos Merkel, when she realizes
who it's from. "Go on." *"I'm taking the liberty
of sending you, along with this letter, a book of
my poems."* "A poet," sighs Merkel, "It's an
awful waste of broad shoulders." "Ever hear
of him?" *"Je n'ai pas."* "Neither have I. Coffee?"

Things to Do in a '70s Disaster Film

Get shaken by an earthquake (in Sensurround).

Flee a swarm of killer bees.

Escape an overturned ocean liner.

Be buried by an avalanche.

Count the minutes before a meteor strikes.

Ignite a bomb in the lavatory of a Boeing 707.

Board the Hindenburg.

Survive a hurricane.

Ride a rollercoaster (in Sensurround).

Wait to be rescued from a burning skyscraper.

On Phone with Elaine

You know me,
I remember everything—
sort of.

Counting My Scars

1) The faint white circle
   on my forehead where
   a wart was removed.

2) The indentation in my left cheek
   (most noticeable when I smile)
   where, as a toddler, I fell and hit
   the corner of our coffee table.

3) The scar on my chin
   I got in high school—
   eight stitches, as I recall.
   After a friend and I smoked
   a joint in his garage,
   I stood up too fast, blacked
   out, and fell chin first
   on the cement floor.
   My friend handed me
   a greasy rag to stop
   the blood pouring down
   my neck. My mother
   found a doctor who
   would see us after hours.
   As he sewed the wound,
   he let me know that he
   knew that I was stoned.

4) The excision on the left side of my neck
   where they took out a pre-cancerous mole.
   Like a child, I rewarded myself afterwards,
   with a plastic glow-in-the-dark candlestick from
   the Museum of Contemporary Art's gift shop.

5) The discolored mark
    in the middle of my left
    ring finger, where my brother
    stabbed me with a pencil.
    We were arguing over whose
    turn it was to sleep in the
    top bunk. I've carried this lead
    with me my entire life.

6) The white cross-shaped scar
    on my left wrist. From the car
    accident in 1979. Where the IV
    was inserted and taped in place.

7) The Frankenstein-esque scar
    down the middle of my stomach,
    also from the accident. From
    the removal of my spleen.

8) Another Frankenstein-esque scar,
    also from the accident, that starts
    in front and wraps around my left side,
    onto my back. From a collapsed lung.

9) The line across my pelvis
    (hidden by pubic hair) from
    the repair of a double hernia.
    In the recovery room, they
    kept making me drink water,
    as they wouldn't release me
    until I peed. It hurt to walk,
    worse to urinate. Climbing

the two flights of stairs to
my loft was one of the most
difficult things I've ever had
to do. I spent a week (at least)
on the couch in the living room,
sleeping and watching movies
on TV. Trust me, *Who's Afraid
of Virginia Woolf?* on Vicodin
is a special kind of insane.

10) The dark crescent—again from
the accident—that runs the length
of my left tibia. The bone, I was
told, "snapped like a branch."
It was mended with a metal plate.
Which they removed a year later.
Before the operation, as I lay on
a gurney, tears streamed down the
side of my face. When he came
to put me under, the doctor wiped
them away and said, "You're very
brave." Then: "You're going to feel
a prick." Which, being gay, made me
laugh. Then everything went black.

Gossip Columnist

It was one of those heedless, luxury-glutted times that usually happens before a disaster. Dorothy, wearing a black felt hat that looked like two crossed bird wings, took out her steno pad and began jotting. Not to be honest, but to be famous. With skin as thin as the rustling outer layer of an onion, she could be inexplicably cool to those whom she was led to believe were in the enemy camp. To be a rival in her field meant eventually not to be in her field at all. He was a sweet and tender man, not at all "Hollywood." When he moved from the Ritz Towers, where he had long lived, it took twenty-six moving vans to carry his furnishings, his mammoth wardrobe, and his two hundred walking sticks. He must have lived within himself a great deal. She bought a cherry-red hat for their day at Santa Anita. The hat was never seen again. Dorothy had no interest in the out-of-doors. She lived her life to music. She had five telephones installed in the apartment. Her dressing room was a poem of feminine fragility, all white wicker with pale pink trimmings. She was in and out of limousines in Ceil Chapman originals and mink. There is one picture of her perusing a nightclub menu through a lorgnette. The camera was no friend to her. The short white gloves that she wore with every outfit had a significance beyond habit. Style was control with grace. Gin and gardenias. A pride of thirties-style wisecracks. A new pink satin or fruit-heavy Sally Victor hat. Her ubiquitous bowed pumps. Though she wore red shoes, her feet were planted firmly on the ground. Richard was a glitter boy. He had a decorator's card and a flair for thematic, sparky, early camp. He had his own stationery done in his favorite color, pumpkin. The danger signs were manifold. He suffered dreadful insomnia, drank and smoked excessively, and had nothing approaching Dorothy's natural vitality. She was out with him almost every night until three or four in the morning. It was a joyless affair with champagne and cake. Dorothy fussed with her pearls. She was no more capable of confronting the wellsprings than she was of dealing with their consequences. It was simply not in her nature. She placed a tiara on her head, put on her white mink cape lined in silver lamé, grabbed some pencils, and she was off to Westminster Abbey.

Isabel Jewell

All but forgotten today, Isabel Jewell appeared, between 1932 and 1972, in over sixty movies, usually in small and uncredited roles. She played stenographers and telephone operators, prison laundry matrons and gun molls, hysterical mothers. Sassy in one part, pitiable in the next, she is best remembered as "that white trash" Emmy Slattery in the now disgraced *Gone With the Wind*—a lesson in the impermanence of prestige. *Whatever became of . . . Isabel Jewell?* Petite and blonde, a pretty girl from Wyoming, she married and divorced three times, and died, by her own hand (barbiturates), at the age of sixty-four. Another lesson in impermanence. Several nights ago, after watching *A Tale of Two Cities*, the 1935 version of Charles Dickens' yarn about the French Revolution, I decided that Isabel Jewell deserved an ode. A petite ode, as enchanting as the sound of her name—that contains both a bell and a jewel. She doesn't appear until the end of the film, as the seamstress condemned to die for simply befriending an aristocrat. Ronald Colman, the star of the picture, comforts her as they're waiting to be carted through the angry mob, inspires her to be brave. At the foot of the guillotine he kisses her farewell. A kiss from Ronald Colman—a matinee idol! O Isabel, how lightly you climbed the steps to your death!

Garbo Talks

(October 1929)

Before dawn, Garbo
walks along the Pacific
coast, her daily (and
as it turned out lifelong) form
of exercise. The movies

are silent no more,
but she has yet to speak. Is
she repeating, to
herself, lines she's memorized,
that she must, in a matter

of hours, perform for
the camera? What will she
sound like? How will the
public react to her thick
accent? Will they turn on her,

the throngs that sit in
the dark and know her, it seems,
better than she knows
herself? She'll have to tone down
gestures, emote in a more

realistic way.
As the world waits, Garbo walks.
(Years to come, stardom
long abandoned—but stalking
her still—she'll spend time trying

to find the perfect
walking shoes.) A limousine,

headlights dimmed, follows
at a respectful distance,
waiting to deliver her

to the studio
so she can deliver, in
her husky Swedish
accent, the first words the world
will hear (a voice, as it turned

out, the throngs adored).
Let them wait. As Garbo walks
briskly. As her scarf
floats like white smoke in the salt
breeze. As the sea repeats, in

the dark, its one line.
When the sky starts to lighten,
the limousine stops.
She turns and strides toward it,
clutching her coat at her throat.

All These Years

I have kept
my Raymond Carver
close to me.

Fun Fact

Elizabeth Bishop saw *Star Wars*.

To Stay Honest

Every now and then
you need a little
Frederick Seidel.

In Old Cartoons

If you are a child of the Great Depression, dressed in rags and always hungry, have no fear. Tonight you can visit Dreamland and shake new clothes, like leaves, off the limbs of a tree. You can pluck a cone from the ice cream patch and pour, from a calla lily, syrup all over it. You'll squeal with delight as you ride an animal cracker on the chocolate merry-go-round cake. And catch, in a buttercup, popcorn falling like snow. If, on the other hand, you find yourself painted on a Dutch plate, no worries. When the grown-ups are asleep, you will come alive and dance, in your wooden shoes, as the beer steins clap their lids in accompaniment. But oh, if you should find yourself in Balloon Land, beware. You're just filled with air and your skin is thin. Lurking in the forest is the Pincushion Man, who wears a thimble for a hat and throws sewing pins like daggers. And whose sole purpose is to pop you!

Made in Hollywood

The rich are always
taking impromptu trips
to Europe—packing
their wardrobe trunks and
waving goodbye from
the decks of luxury liners
as streamers rain down
around them. They're
always drinking bootleg
gin and frolicking on
somebody or other's
millionaire father's
festively lit yacht. Or
being ferried out
to a gambling ship
(run by gangsters)
anchored in the harbor.
For some, the Depression
is the best of times.
The women wear
clinging evening gowns
that look more like
satin slips, jewels
dripping from them
like tinsel. The men
wear tails, pull cigarettes
from engraved cases,
and bet all of it—
mountainous stacks
of chips—on roulette.
Meanwhile, our heroine
(who is really poor)
stands alone on deck.

We see her from the
back: blonde hair, fur
wrap, an ocean of
shimmering black silk.
She leans against the rail,
full moon frozen above
her like a silver coin,
wondering how long
she can keep up this
pretense of extravagance,
what with a threadbare
mother and younger
sister at home. For
others, the Depression
is the worst of times. But
everyone loves the
movies. Who wouldn't
squander that moon,
as if it were their last
quarter, for a few
hours of make-believe
in a dark theater?

Written After Reading Jerome Sala's "How Much?"

In a group photo
taken at a Ramones
concert at the Savoy
in San Francisco in
1976, I wear a tacky
sweater and hold
a book, the title of
which I can't make
out. I always had
a book with me in
those days. But who
brings a book to a
punk rock concert?
And where is it now,
this book that I hold so
close to my heart?

Photo I Didn't Post on Instagram

Struck by pink on a walk

The Fear of Masculinity

Finally, one night in Chicago,
quite unexpectedly, I understood.
I've been out since my late teens,
but it took two women, over three
decades later, to enlighten me. I was
having dinner at a Thai restaurant
with my colleague Lisa Fishman
and Jennifer Moxley, who'd flown
from Maine to give a poetry reading
at Columbia College. I forget
the context, but at some point
in the conversation I said, "I've
never understood why straight
men hate homosexuals so much."
Both women, facing me across
the table, looked mildly surprised.
As if it were no mystery to them.
"Well," said Lisa, "in their eyes
one of the men would have to be
the woman." It wasn't enough
to make the lightbulb go off. So
Jennifer added, pointedly, "And
nothing could be worse than that."

Movies That Make Me Cry

The Best Years of Our Lives (1946)

Casablanca (1942)

Cold Mountain (2003)

Dances with Wolves (1990)

The Deep End of the Ocean (1999)

Field of Dreams (1989)

The Ghost and Mrs. Muir (1947)

Hostiles (2017)

It's a Wonderful Life (1946)

The Lives of Others (2006)

Manchester by the Sea (2016)

The Miracle Worker (1962)

Ordinary People (1980)

Pollyanna (1960)

The Secret in Their Eyes (2009)

The Sound of Music (1965)

True Grit (2010)

The Virgin Spring (1960)

The Prom Dress Thief

for Camille Guthrie

One by one, prom dresses began to disappear from the girls'
dormitory rooms. Who was stealing them, and why? Naturally
the girls were distraught at this rash of thefts. Their strapless,
full-skirted satin gowns—pink, yellow, aqua, lavender—overlaid
with tulle and layers of lace ruffles, were precious flowers they
would press between the pages of a book of poetry, if they could.
At last, the thief was found out, a girl whose dorm room was
filthy with formals: prom dresses under her bed, prom dresses
stuffed in her closet. The girls, as you can imagine, were relieved
to retrieve their precious dresses (even though they were destined
for attic or thrift shop). It is not known what punishment was
meted out to the culprit for her crimes.

This occurred at Smith College in Northampton, Massachusetts,
in the early 1950s. Sylvia Plath was a student there at the time. In
a letter, she waxed poetic about the dress she wore to the Junior
Prom: "silvery top-winged softly, with a tiny high waist and a
swoosh of white net with a very palish lavendar [*sic*] overtone!"
Blessedly, it did not fall prey to a prom dress thief. Today Plath's
"exquisite formal" is housed in an archive at her alma mater, and
is considered a piece of historical clothing.

Match the Bird with the Poet

Black Rook   Edgar Allan Poe

Bobolink   Bernadette Mayer

Crow   John Keats

Nightingale   W.B. Yeats

Ostrich   Ted Hughes

Raven   Sylvia Plath

Sandpiper   Percy Bysshe Shelley

Scarlet Tanager   Emily Dickinson

Skylark   Elizabeth Bishop

Swan   Marianne Moore

Movie Briefs

1

Smart Woman (1931)

A gem of a movie, deftly handled
by Gregory La Cava (who will
direct the classic *My Man Godfrey*
five years later). But a shock
to learn, when I consulted Wikipedia
afterwards, that the lead actor,
Robert Ames, was found dead
in a New York hotel room just two
months after *Smart Woman* was
released. Age forty-two. Ames
was an alcoholic; the cause of his
death was attributed to "his
sudden abstinence from alcohol."

Also shocking to learn that his
co-star, character actress Gladys
Gale, who plays the mother of
a woman Ames is having an
affair with, was found dead in
a Los Angeles hotel room in 1948.
Age fifty-seven. She and a man
had checked in under assumed
names (Mr. and Mrs. Statler);
the following morning her nude
body was discovered. The man
gone. Hotel room trashed. No
cause of death ever established.

2

Let Us Be Gay (1930)

The most interesting thing about
this movie is we get to see Norma
Shearer as a dowdy housewife—
shapeless smock, curlers, no
make-up. After the housewife
divorces her unfaithful husband,
she of course gets glamorized.
Also of interest: She plays the
mother of two young children
(like Shearer herself); she'll later
turn down the role of Mrs. Miniver
(for which Greer Garson would
win an Oscar) because vanity
would not permit her to be seen
as the mother of a young man.
(Greer would marry the much
younger actor who played her son.)
After she retired from acting
in 1942 (she did not care to age
onscreen), Shearer married
a ski instructor ten years her
junior. Terrified of old age
(what she will die of, in 1983),
Norma would take ice baths
in the middle of the night, to
tighten her skin. When a clerk
at a drugstore recognized her—
"Aren't you Norma Shearer?"—
she denied that she was herself.

3

The Captain Hates the Sea (1934)

The final film of John Gilbert,
matinee idol who had successfully
transitioned to sound four years
earlier, after fifteen years in silents.
His voice was rich and resonant,
but MGM mogul Louis B. Mayer,
unhappy with Gilbert's high salary,
reportedly had his voice distorted.
Thus the "squeaky voice" myth.
By the time he made *The Captain
Hates the Sea* at Columbia, Gilbert
had nearly succeeded in drinking
himself to death. (He would die
a little more than a year later,
at the age of thirty-eight, after
suffering a heart attack brought
on by his alcoholism.) Described
as *Grand Hotel* on a cruise ship,
the film went over budget due to
the nightly carousing of the four
male leads: Gilbert, Victor McLaglen,
Walter Connolly, and Walter Catlett.
Alarmed, Columbia head Harry Cohn
cabled director Lewis Milestone:
"Hurry up! The cost is staggering!"
Milestone cabled back: "So is the cast!"

4

Mystery of the Wax Museum (1933)

The grisly horror classic, filmed
in the primitive two-strip Tech-
nicolor process—an unreal palette
of red-orange and blue-green.
Once considered lost, the movie
has been restored to its original
splendor (by the UCLA Film &
Television Archive) and released
on Blu-ray and DVD. From the audio
commentary, I learn that Allen
Vincent (who plays Fay Wray's
love interest) was in fact gay,
and that at Hollywood parties,
Humphrey Bogart, "always the
belligerent drunk, would bully
the gentle actor for his homo-
sexuality." Due to a hearing
impairment, Vincent eventually
switched from acting to screen-
writing. (He'd garner an Oscar
nomination, in 1948, for his
script of *Johnny Belinda*, about
the rape of a "deaf mute," played
by Jane Wyman.) Gavin Gordon,
another actor in *Mystery of the
Wax Museum*, was also gay.
From the South, Gordon had
a suave, slightly sinister de-
meanor. A half-century later, he
and Vincent would both die,
four years apart, in Canoga Park,

California. Were they partners? I
have no proof, but I'd like to
think they lived out their elder
years with each other, basking
in glamorous memories. They
appear together in another film,
Two Against the World (1932),
and can be seen crossing a ball-
room, in between the waltzing
heterosexual couples, arm in arm.

5

Possessed (1931)

Terrific pre-Code drama with
Joan Crawford and Clark Gable,
the third of eight movies they
made together. Joan rises from
rags to riches (as was her wont).
An actress I'd never heard of,
Marjorie White—short, blonde,
grating Jersey accent—has a small
but memorable part as "a cheap
little tramp" who crashes Joan's
elegant dinner party. White's
career was cut short on August 20,
1935, in Santa Monica, California:
She was riding in a convertible
driven by one Marlow M. Lovell
that sideswiped the car of a couple
who'd been married only one hour
before. Lovell's car overturned (his
reckless driving was deemed the
cause of the accident). White was
the only person seriously injured.
She died of internal hemorrhaging
the next day, age thirty-one. All
told, she appeared in a dozen films.

Another actress, Clara Blandick,
makes a brief appearance early in
the movie, as Joan's mother. She'll
achieve the kind of immortality
White was denied when, eight years
later, she'll play Auntie Em in *The*

Wizard of Oz. In 1962, her eyesight
failing and suffering from acute
arthritis pain, she'll end her own
life. Dressed in a royal blue gown,
hair immaculately styled, she'll
take an overdose of sleeping pills,
lie down on her couch, cover herself
with a gold blanket, and tie a plastic
bag over her head. In her suicide
note she'll write: "I am now about
to make the great adventure."

6

Ready, Willing, and Able (1937)

A rather dull musical comedy,
but worth it for the grand finale
alone: Ruby Keeler tap-dancing on
the keys of a gigantic typewriter.
Busby Berkeley couldn't have done
better. I watched it so I could see
Ross Alexander, a contract player at
Warner Brothers in the 1930s, who
I'd read was a tormented closet case.
Wavy black hair, boyish good looks,
deep voice (to mask his homosexual-
ity?), always energetic and cheerful.
Also wrote poetry (a dead giveaway).
Ross co-starred with Errol Flynn in
Captain Blood; rumors had it that they
had an affair during the making of
the film. He appeared in seventeen
movies in five years; *Ready, Willing,
and Able* was his last. His first wife,
actress Aleta Freel, committed suicide
by shooting herself in the head; her
career had stalled, while Ross' had
skyrocketed. Although devastated,
he then married actress Anne Nagel.
Three months later, alcoholic, in
debt, and deeply closeted, Ross said
he was going out to the barn on his
Hollywood estate to write poetry
and instead shot himself in the head
with the same gun his first wife had
used to kill herself. He was twenty-

nine years of age. Before the police
were called, representatives from
the studio arrived to confiscate any
incriminating papers. Ross' poems,
among them, were never seen again.

7

Weary River (1929)

This transitional talkie (half
silent, half sound), a prison yarn
starring the soulful Richard
Barthelmess, led me to Betty
Compson, his co-star, an actress
whose career spanned the years
1915 to 1948 (most of her silent
movies are lost), who led me to
Milton Sills, with whom she
appeared in several films, a
matinee idol in the silent era
who was married to Doris Kenyon,
with whom he often co-starred,
who led me to *The Sea Hawk* (1924),
Sills' biggest box office success,
the only film of his available on
DVD, an adventure on the high
seas (why do silent movies always
put me to sleep?), and who also
led me (this is a kind of sidebar)
to John H. Collins, director of
the 1919 silent comedy *Satan Junior*,
starring Sills and Collins' wife
Viola Dana, during the filming
of which he died of the 1918 influ-
enza epidemic (age twenty-eight),
and (back to Sills) ultimately led
me to a poem by Weldon Kees (the
poet who, in 1955, disappeared at
the age of forty-one, most likely
having jumped from the Golden

Gate Bridge), "1926" (one of the
earliest poems I know of that al-
ludes to movie stars), in which
the twelve-year-old speaker has
just seen a film with Milton Sills
(Kees' favorite actor as a boy), and
which inspired my poem "1968,"
about my love of movies as a teen.

Milton Sills died unexpectedly in
1930, of a heart attack, age forty-
eight, while playing tennis with
his wife Doris at their Brentwood
home. After his death, a poem
Sills had written was discovered
among his personal effects. A love
poem to his wife. Which begins
"Death cannot end all things . . ."

The Ten Greatest Books of the Year (2022)

after Ted Berrigan

Pure Pagan: Seven Centuries of Greek Poems and Fragments
Kimiko Hahn, Mosquito & Ant
Mark A. Vieira, Sin in Soft Focus: Pre-Code Hollywood
Alice Notley, Doctor Williams' Heiresses
Maxine Scates, My Wilderness
Henri Lefebvre, The Missing Pieces
Thomas Doherty, Pre-Code Hollywood: Sex, Immorality, and
    Insurrection in American Cinema, 1930-1934
Richard Wright, Haiku: The Last Poems of an American Icon
James Thomas Stevens, The Golden Book
Liz Hockinson, Marcello the Movie Mouse
Matthew Burgess, Flesh, Farewell
Jack Skelley, Interstellar Theme Park: New and Selected Writing
Sidney D. Kirkpatrick, A Cast of Killers
Jack Kerouac, Albert Saijo & Lew Welch, Trip Trap: Haiku on
    the Road
Herodotus, The Histories
Frederick Seidel, These Days
Euripides, The Heracleidae
Janet Gray, A Hundred Flowers
Raymond Carver, Ultramarine
Cyril Connolly, The Unquiet Grave
The Ink Dark Moon: Love Poems by Ono no Komachi and
    Ixumi Shikibu, Women of the Ancient Court of Japan
Sandra Simonds, 11 Triptychs
Jerome Sala, How Much?: New and Selected Poems
Robert Lowell, Imitations
Michael Robins, The Bright Invisible
William Shakespeare, A Midsummer Night's Dream
James Cushing, Tangled Hologram
Eugenio Montale, Selected Poems
Ted Berrigan, Get the Money!: Collected Prose (1961-1983)

D.A. Powell, Low Hanging Fruit
John Yau, Joe Brainard: The Art of the Personal
Ted Berrigan, In the Early Morning Rain
Ted Berrigan, Nothing for You
Joel Oppenheimer, In Time: Poems 1962-1968
Ted Berrigan, Red Wagon
Ted Berrigan, Train Ride
Bernadette Mayer, Milkweed Smithereens
Ron Padgett, Dot
Ted Berrigan, A Certain Slant of Sunlight
Aeschylus, The Persians
Alex Katz: Gathering
Max Jacob, The Dice Cup
Arthur Rimbaud, Complete Works

Blonde

I used to be brunette,
But now I am blonde.

I used to be a starlet,
But now I am a serious actress.

I used to want my mother's love,
But now I love the camera.

I used to want my father's love,
But now I marry powerful men.

I used to speak for myself,
But now I am a female impersonator.

I used to be pregnant,
But now I am myself a child.

I used to bask in the spotlight,
But now I keep them waiting on the set.

I used to reach for pills, for champagne,
But now my handprints are solidified in cement.

I used to exist,
But now I am the subject of a sexist bio-pic.

I used to pose nude,
But now I am naked.

Fall

A Post-it

    fluttered down

        like a yellow leaf

On Phone with Doug

2:00 a.m.

Remember how in the seventies there was a whole slew of Sherlock Holmes movies?

Yes, that's right.

There was *The Private Life of Sherlock Holmes*, directed by Billy Wilder. And *They Might Be Giants*, with George C. Scott and Joanne Woodward. Scott thinks he's Sherlock Holmes and Woodward is a psychiatrist named Dr. Watson.

I love that movie.

Me, too. I just got it on Blu-ray.

There was *The Seven-Per-Cent Solution*.

Yes. Sherlock Holmes meets Freud. Who played Holmes?

I'm googling it.

I saw it when it came out.

Nicol Williamson. Alan Arkin plays Freud. It also has Vanessa Redgrave and Laurence Olivier and Samantha Eggar. What a cast. It even has Joel Grey!

What was the one where Sherlock Holmes meets Jack the Ripper?

Time After Time.

No, that was H.G. Wells meets Jack the Ripper. With Malcom McDowell and Mary Steenburgen. I recently rewatched it on HBO.

Then there was *Sherlock Holmes' Smarter Brother*. Gene Wilder, Marty Feldman, Madeline Kahn, Dom DeLuise. You probably wouldn't like it.

I'm not big on Gene Wilder.

And Mel Brooks.

Him, either. Or any of those corny comedians. Madeline Kahn excluded, of course. But what was the one where Sherlock Holmes meets Jack the Ripper?

Time After Time.

No, that's H.G. Wells meets Jack the Ripper.

Oh, right. I'll look it up. Sherlock Holmes meets Jack the Ripper . . . *Murder by Decree.*

That's it.

From 1979. With Christopher Plummer as Holmes and James Mason as Watson. And Donald Sutherland and Geneviève Bujold.

James Mason is great, isn't he.

James Mason is always good.

But he never won an Oscar, did he.

No. Life just isn't fair.

From an Unfinished Letter to Jennifer Moxley

August 1, 2019

1.

I'm in the middle of cleaning up my office (so many little stacks
of papers and books) and the urge to write to you just came over
me, so I'm taking a break to say hello. But first I'm going to
prepare some cantaloupe. Five minutes later: back with a plate
of sweet orange slices—taste I never tire of, that always takes me
back to childhood, to that pink kitchen in Chatsworth. (Just bit
my lip, damnit, I obviously can't eat cantaloupe and type at the
same time.)

> *scooping out the seeds*
> *forever pink in memory*

2.

I was on the go after we missed seeing each other in Boston. I
went to California twice. First, two weeks in May with family.
My father is almost ninety and becoming more and more frail,
so I wanted to go and spend time with him. All four children
were there at one point: me, two sisters, older brother. The first
time we were all together since my mother died in 1996. It was
lovely, actually. No major upsets. Played cards at night—Hearts,
Michigan Rummy. I haven't spoken much with my brother my
entire adult life, so when he left and said "I love you," I was
floored. Linda, my sister from Atlanta (she lost her husband
about six months ago) left earlier than planned because her
daughter was giving birth to twins in North Carolina. Some
nice moments used book shopping with my sisters. At a store
in Atascadero, Linda came across one of my books and said to
the owner, "This is by my brother, he's an author." I heard her

and turned red. "Have him sign it," he said. But Linda bought it instead. I did a class visit/reading at Cal Poly while there (it's an hour north of Nipomo, where my father lives). As I was preparing to leave, my father made a point of telling me, in the hall, that he hoped the reading went well and that the students got something out of it. Nothing short of a miracle, if you knew my father.

it took the poet by surprise to get
what he must have always wanted

3.

I flew back to California the following month. The Ed Smith book was just out, so we did group events in Los Angeles (at Beyond Baroque) and in San Francisco (at City Lights). Both events couldn't have gone better: well-attended, Ed's work read by his friends and appreciated by audiences. After the L.A. reading, Amy Gerstler and I drove up the coast, stopping for an hour to say hello to my father and sister. Just enough time to go to the bathroom and make a peanut butter and jelly sandwich for the road. And for Amy to meet them and pet their dogs. We stayed at a hotel in Chinatown. Kevin, who was scheduled to read with us at City Lights, had just died. To my surprise, Dodie (who was also on the lineup) reached out and wanted to meet me before the reading. We had coffee, then dinner. She was surprisingly held together (she said people were telling her that she was in shock), talked freely about Kevin's illness and death, was only upset by the way some people were immediately planning memorial events without consulting her. Their proprietary (and probably careerist) attitude, as if death had left Kevin up for grabs. When Kevin was diagnosed with a brain tumor, he said he thought the cause was a lifetime of being nice to people he didn't like. Dodie said he had started telling people what he really thought. She read the poems Kevin was going to read; it was moving. A group of us went out to eat afterwards—Dodie, Doug Powell, Randy Mann, Amy, Roberto Bedoya, Diane Ward (who I hadn't seen in decades), etc. Everything was moving so fast it hardly computed that I was at City Lights bookstore, that Ed's poetry was being read and received positively (lots of laughs, but also incredibly moving at times). The next day Dodie emailed and thanked me, said the night out was just what she needed.

the dead are speechless
without our grief

4.

Amy and I drove back to Los Angeles through the San Joaquin Valley. I was reading to her out loud—Emily Dickinson's niece's gorgeous memoir about her aunt—and at one point looked up: The mountains at the southern end of the valley were covered with a blanket of purple wildflowers. Really beautiful. I burst into tears—all the built-up emotion of the trip triggered by those purple hills and Emily's complicated feelings about her mother.

my mother's favorite color
was lavender

I've been reading Elizabeth Bishop's letters again, they're really
addictive. She's fairly unguarded. Shook up by Dylan Thomas'
death (in November 1953), she writes (to Robert Lowell): *"Why
do some poets manage to get by and live to be malicious old
bores like Frost or—probably—pompous old ones like Yeats,
or crazy old ones like Pound—and some just don't."* Elsewhere
she calls Frost "the Bad Gray Poet." The gossip is great, but her
descriptions of life in Brazil in the '50s and '60s are marvelous.
I've also been dipping into the letters of Dickinson and Plath, but,
for the moment, Bishop is winning. Of course the letters lead to
poems: Bishop's, Lowell's, Marianne Moore's. She herself loved
letters, read all of Coleridge's when they were published. Have
you ever read his? Not that I need another tome. Not when the
two-volume Nathaniel Hawthorne diary is waiting for me. His
descriptions are to die for as well. I bought the set at the Strand
in New York a trip or two ago, because I opened one volume to a
description of "frost-feathers" on trees on an icy March morning
(in 1845) and had to have them. At the end of a long description
of these ice-covered trees, he says, "All the above description is
most unsatisfactory." Why are we so hard on ourselves!

*"perhaps a subdued glow will do something
towards the expression of it"*

Sonnet Bernadette Mayer

Even when you have nothing to do there's
Too much history to put into poetry
Is the work to be done in secret or out loud?
I've chosen to grow old awkwardly, like a teenager

A full blast of sun is on the shirt on a hanger
We saw a brilliantly red tree in Rayville
Now the leaves are rushing off the yellow tree
The gingko hasn't done any of its autumn tricks yet

My favorite thing to do is to watch a volcano erupt
It goes like popcorn at the million dollar movie
The idea that writing is easy comes from Frank O'Hara
Gods & philosophies inevitably let you down

I'll be sorry for writing this poem (if it is a poem)
Some pleasure might be taken in a new color

Stolen Jewels

Automats
Bellboys
Wall safes
Roulette wheels
Shooting galleries
Chauffeurs
Telegrams
Staterooms
Full moons
Seances

Carole Lombard

At the end of one of her movies (*No More Orchids*, 1932), her father (played by Walter Connolly) flies his airplane into the side of a mountain. We see a brief explosion, shattered fuselage. An image difficult to take, knowing it will be her fate ten years later. A death unbefitting (as if we have a say in the matter) this shimmering blonde beacon of the silver screen. "Survived by all of us," is how Frank O'Hara, himself a tragic figure, put it. (*In Chicago today it's raining.*) Screwball heiress, phony princess, small town librarian, gold-digging chorus girl—all her roles sparkle with her inimitable quick-wittedness. She held her own with the leading men of the time: Gary Cooper, William Powell (husband number one), John Barrymore, Fredric March, Clark Gable (husband number two), James Stewart, Cary Grant. At age eighteen, a car accident nearly ended her career—glass from a smashed windshield left a scar on her cheek. (You can see it in close-ups.) A scar keep her from becoming a star? *Not on your life, buster.* When the United States entered World War II, Lombard traveled to Indiana, her home state, where, in a single evening, she raised over two million dollars in defense bonds. Instead of returning to Hollywood by train, as planned, Lombard decided to fly. (She had quarreled with Gable before the trip, and wanted to make haste.) On the evening of January 16, 1942, her plane crashed into the side of a mountain southwest of Las Vegas. All twenty-two souls on board, including Lombard and her mother, perished. Lombard had recently completed filming the Ernst Lubitsch anti-Nazi black comedy *To Be or Not to Be.* By the time it was released, one month after her death, fate had already answered the question.

Her Afterlife

Carole Lombard doing the rumba
    with George Raft
in a dress made of starlight.

The beautiful

silveriness

of rain in

black and white

Difficult to Win Over by Enchantments

from the Ancient Greek

fallen from heaven
twenty years old
lovely
with bright eyes
with trailing robe
overlaid with silver
ornament
fix on with a brooch
adorn with garlands
be lost in passion
nine nights long

[*several lines gone*]

plume of a helmet
raise the war cry
fight in vain
stain with blood
call down curses upon
fear
casting a long shadow
most miserable
driven on by bad winds
hated by the gods
utter ruin
woe!

The Poems Attributed to Him May Be by Different Poets

He lived in the time of Alexander the Great, to whose death he
    alludes.
His extant poems are chiefly about country life and hunting.
He is often described as the father of tragedy.
Only seven of his estimated seventy to ninety plays have survived.
It seems probable that his parents, though poor, were respectable.
The work survives, but seems incomplete.
The *Greek Anthology* contains an epigram which is probably the work
    of this flatterer.
He was an older contemporary and an alleged lover of Sappho, with
    whom he may have exchanged poems.
Some of his poems are on literary themes, but most are political.
His report describes accurately the characteristic sequence of
    earthquake, retreat of the sea, and sudden giant wave.
His widespread popularity inspired countless imitators, which also
    kept his name alive.
Described by contemporaries as "a terrible fellow to coin strange
    words."
Scarcely anything is known of his life.
He is associated with the Seven Wonders of the Ancient World,
    which he described in a poem composed about 140 B.C.
Known for being the first to mention use of the waterwheel in a
    poem.
More of her work survives than any other ancient Greek woman, with
    the exception of Sappho.
A crater on the Moon is named in his honor.
A man of taste and elegance, yet deficient in gravity and energy,
    which prevented his writings acquiring that popularity which
    they otherwise deserved, and may have been one of the causes of
    their neglect and loss to us.
The majority of his work that has survived is love songs.
One night in 191 A.D., they kidnapped him and threatened to kill
    him if he did not stop writing.

His career as a poet probably benefited from the high reputation of his uncle.

All of his works are lost and are only known by their titles through quotes by later authors.

He especially excelled in descriptions dealing with such subjects as flowers and female beauty.

He is not usually ranked among the top tier of Latin poets, but his writing is elegant, he tells a story well, and his polemical passages occasionally attain an unmatchable level of entertaining vitriol.

There is no reason to suppose he ever lived anywhere other than Alexandria.

He had a daughter who found fame as a poet, composing riddles in hexameter verse.

His brother was an epic poet.

Swaggering soldiers, verbose cooks, courtesans, and parasites, all feature in the fragments.

About 550 lines of his poetry survive, although because ancient writers rarely mentioned which poem they were quoting, it is not always certain to which poem the quotes belong.

An epigram on an ageing vine is attributed to him.

Her poem has been deemed important for the glimpse it gives us of a girl's view of her relationship with her mother.

He was apparently, although obscure, well respected.

He spent much of his life in Athens, where he amassed great wealth.

He is known to have written some erotic verses.

Most of his epigrams are in praise of wine, and all of them are jocular.

He seems to have been a poet of some celebrity.

Some ancient scholars believed him to have been an eyewitness to the Trojan War.

He was greatly admired, chiefly, it would seem, for a sort of elegant wit.

Although he became quite famous after his death, he was only able to earn a bare subsistence from his poetry during his lifetime.

Best known for his characteristic tongue-in-cheek style, with which
he frequently ridiculed superstition, religious practices, and belief
in the paranormal.
The popularity which he enjoyed in his own time is attested by the
fact that at his death, although he had filled none of the offices of
state, he received the honor of a public funeral.
The most famous of his poems opens "Love is not . . ."
The year of his death is not known.
He typically describes himself not as an active and engaged lover, but
as one struck by the beauty of a woman or boy.
A total of fifteen poems are known.
The time he lived is not certain.
He wrote short poems suitable for performance at drinking parties.
She wrote a hymn to Poseidon.
Two other poems, attributed to him at one time or another but no
longer thought to be his, are commonly edited with his work.
Although his fame was great during his lifetime, little survives of his
poetry today.
A large proportion of his epigrams are directed against doctors.
Her epigrams were inspired by Sappho, whom she claims to rival.
His poems are bitter about his wife to the point of misogyny.
He died in Athens, nearly a hundred years old, but with mental vigor
unimpaired, about the year 262 B.C., according to the story, at
the moment of his being crowned on stage.
His epigrams are generally rather dull.
Some ambiguity surrounds his name.
He traveled in Greece, Italy and Asia, reciting his poems.
In his hands the dithyramb seems to have been a sort of comic opera,
and the music, composed by himself, of a debased character.
Aristotle found cause to quote him.
His existence is unclear.
His entire work is believed to have survived intact for over 2,400
years.

He wrote only about drinking and love.

She probably wrote around 10,000 lines of poetry, of which only about 650 survive.

His fame as a poet rests largely on his ability to present basic human situations with affecting simplicity.

He is the earliest Greek poet who claims explicitly to be writing for future generations.

To Light Her Path

If the legend that
this was her final poem
is true, the last word
she wrote was "moon."

ACKNOWLEDGMENTS

Thanks to the editors of the following publications, in which some of the poems in this book were previously published: *Allium, The American Poetry Review, Ariadne, The Best American Poetry 2023* and *2025, BlazeVox, The Brooklyn Rail, Court Green, Elderly, Essential Queer Voices of U.S. Poetry, MumberMag, Plume, Poem-a-Day, Poetry, R&R, Unwoven Literary & Arts Magazine.*